Jesus IS A-MAZE-ING

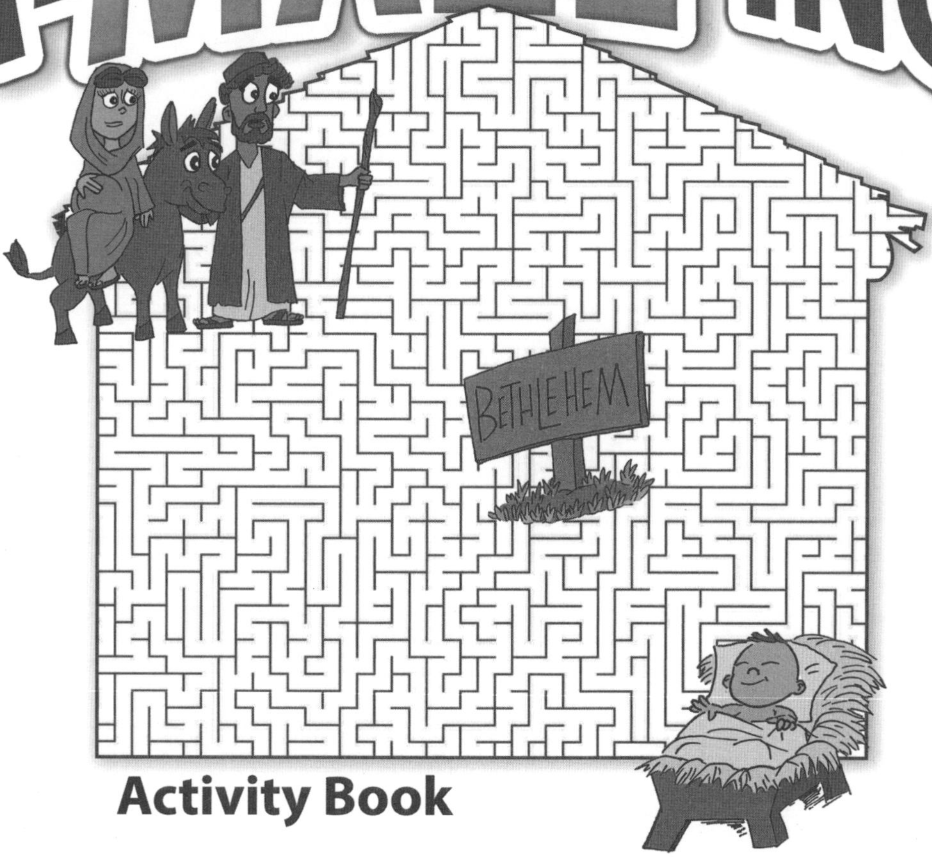

Activity Book

Written by Robin Loisch
Illustrated by Tyler McCorkle

305800232025

The **A-MAZE-ING** Birth of Jesus

God had a wonderful plan to send His only Son to the world. God chose a young woman named Mary to be the baby's mother. Joseph would be the baby's earthly father, but God was the baby's real father. Mary and Joseph obeyed God. They traveled to Bethlehem, and God's Son, Jesus, was born.

Help Mary and Joseph reach Baby Jesus. Watch out for roadblocks along the way!

The **A-MAZE-ING** Baptism of Jesus

John the Baptist preached that God would send a Savior soon. He baptized people who repented of their sins. One day Jesus asked John to baptize Him. John knew Jesus should be baptizing him instead, but he did as Jesus asked. Then the Holy Spirit came down as a dove. God said, "This is my Son, whom I love; with him I am well pleased."

Help Jesus reach John the Baptist. Don't get caught in the lily pads!

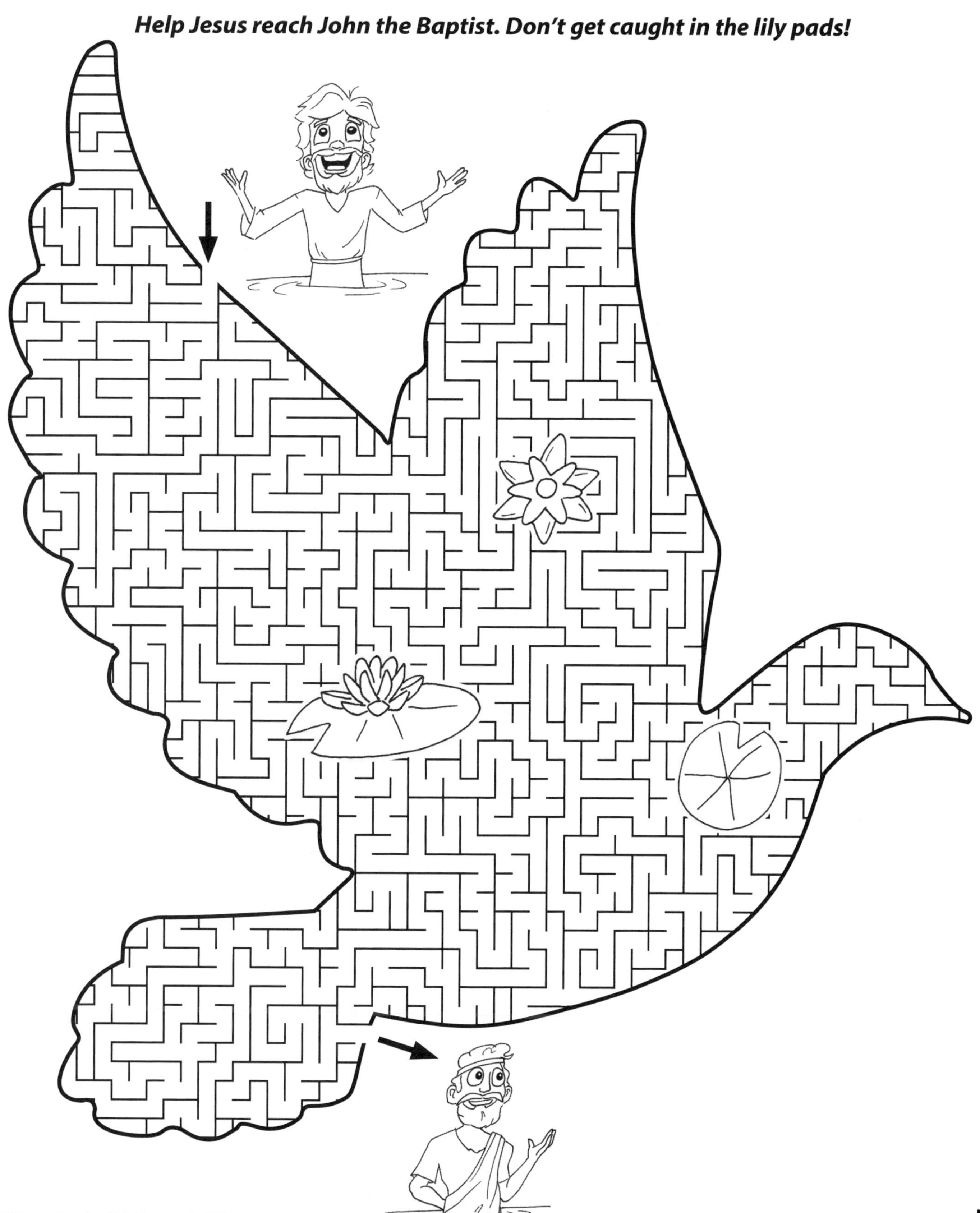

The **A-MAZE-ING** Miracle

At a wedding, Mary told Jesus, "They have no more wine." She told the servants to do whatever Jesus said. Nearby were six large water jars. Jesus said, "Fill the jars with water." Then Jesus said to take some to the master of the banquet. The master tasted it and discovered Jesus had changed the water into wine. This was Jesus' first miracle.

Help Mary reach Jesus. Don't trip on the jars!

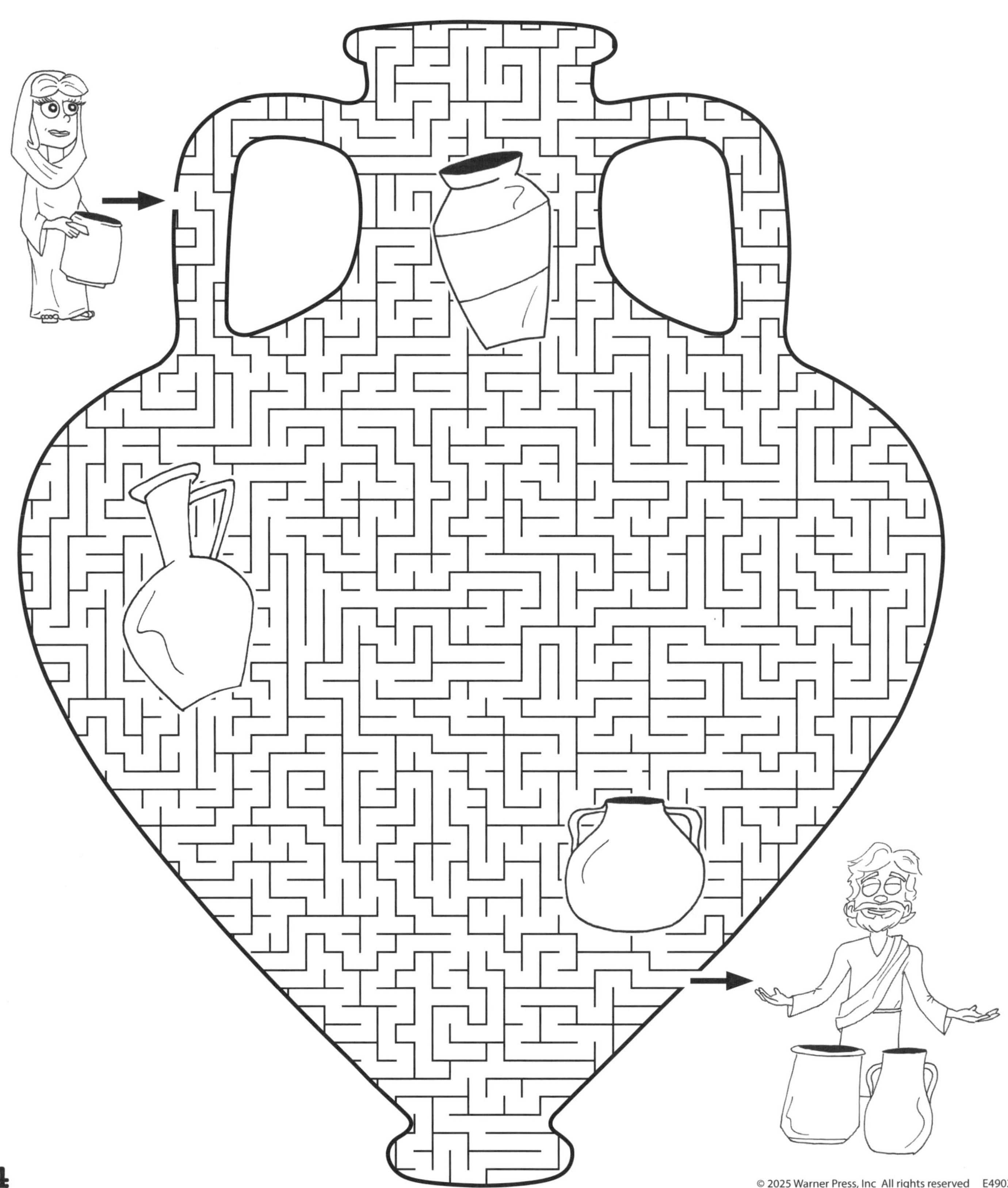

The **A-MAZE-ING** Conversation

Jesus stopped by a well in Samaria to rest. A woman came to get water, and Jesus asked for a drink. The woman was shocked that Jesus spoke to her. Soon she was even more surprised to hear that He knew all about her life. The woman believed Jesus was the Messiah and told everyone about Him. Many other Samaritans became believers too.

Help Jesus reach the woman. Watch out for rocks!

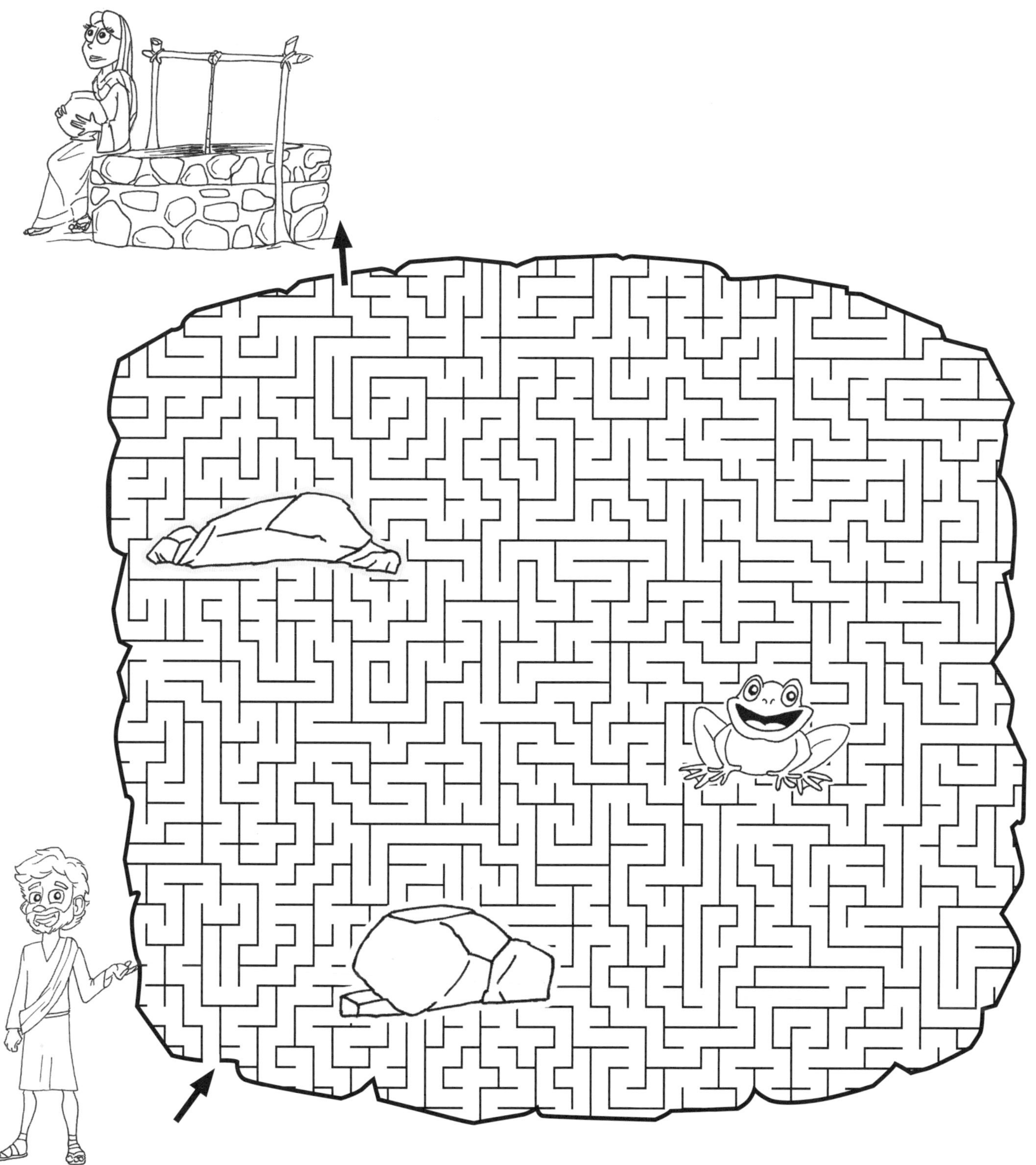

The **A-MAZE-ING** Catch

Jesus taught the people from Simon's boat. (Simon will later be renamed Peter.) Afterwards, He told Simon to go into deep water and lower his nets. Simon said, "We didn't catch any fish all night, but we'll try again if you say so." Soon the nets held so many fish that the boats almost sank! Jesus said, "From now on you will fish for people."

Help Simon reach Jesus. Watch out for the fishhook!

The **A-MAZE-ING** Storm

Jesus and His disciples got on a boat, and Jesus went to sleep. A terrible storm came while they were out on the lake. Waves were crashing over the boat, and the disciples were afraid they would drown. They woke Jesus and said, "Save us!" Jesus rebuked the wind and waves, and the storm stopped. The disciples were amazed!

Help the disciples reach Jesus. Don't be afraid of the storm!

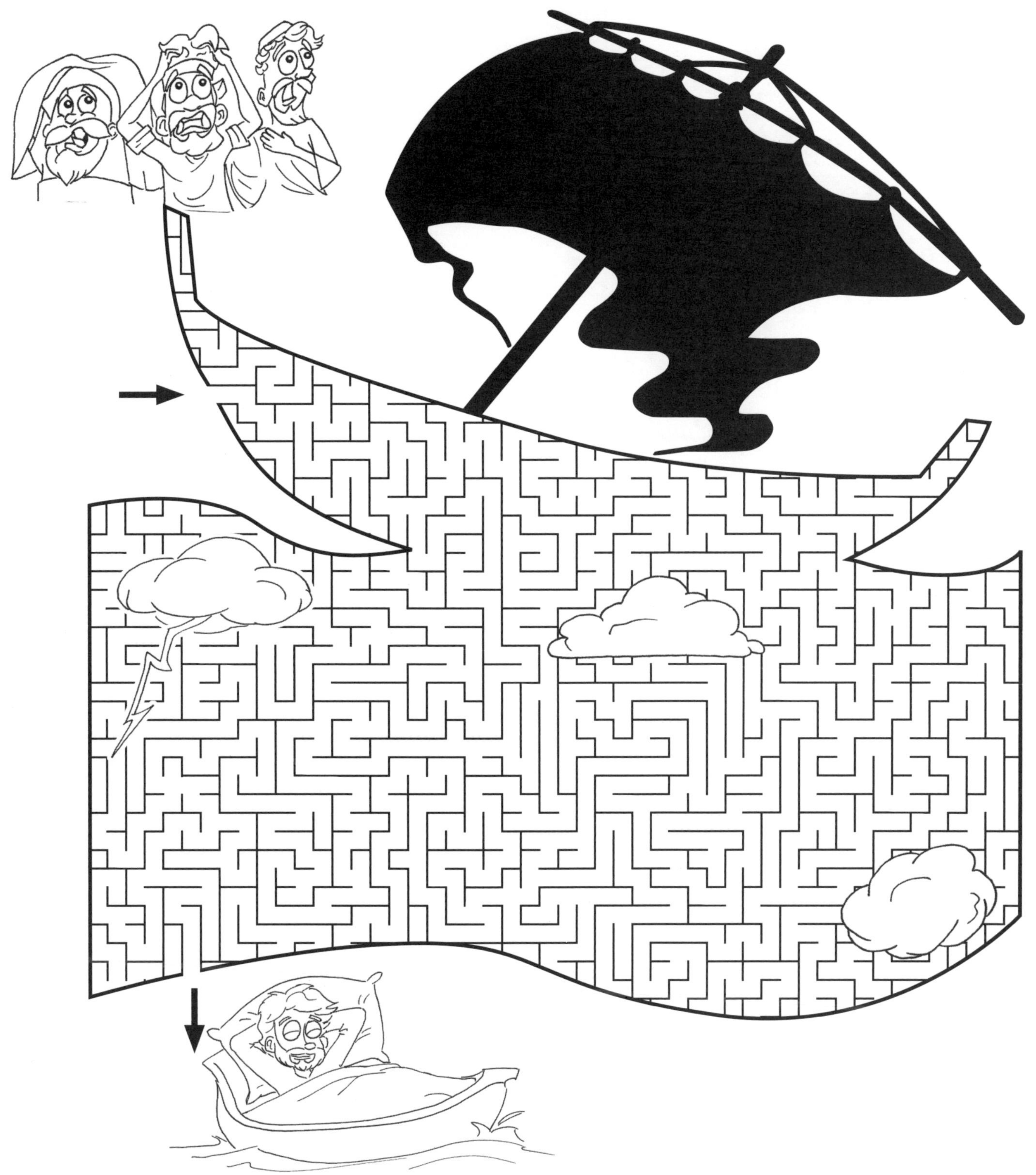

The **A-MAZE-ING** Lunch

Crowds followed Jesus to hear Him preach and to see Him heal the sick. When it was time to eat, no one had the money to buy enough food for 5,000 men. A boy gave Jesus his five small loaves of bread and two small fish. Jesus prayed, the disciples passed out the food, and everyone had enough to eat. They even had 12 baskets of leftovers!

Help the boy take his lunch to Jesus. Don't drop the fish and bread on your way there!

The **A-MAZE-ING** Lesson

A rich young man asked Jesus how to get to heaven. Jesus said, "Keep the commandments." The man said he had been. Then Jesus told the man to sell his things and follow Him. The young man went away sad because he did not want to give up his things. Jesus said, "It is easier for a camel to go through the eye of a needle than for someone rich to enter the kingdom of God."

Help the rich young man find Jesus. Be careful not to stumble on the riches!

The **A-MAZE-ING** Visit

Zacchaeus was a rich tax collector. He was also short. When he heard Jesus was coming, he climbed a tree to see better. He was shocked when Jesus stopped and said, “Zacchaeus, come down. I’m going to your house today.” That visit with Jesus changed Zacchaeus’ life. He gave back all the extra money he had taken and more besides!

Help Zacchaeus climb down the tree to Jesus. Don’t fall for the money!

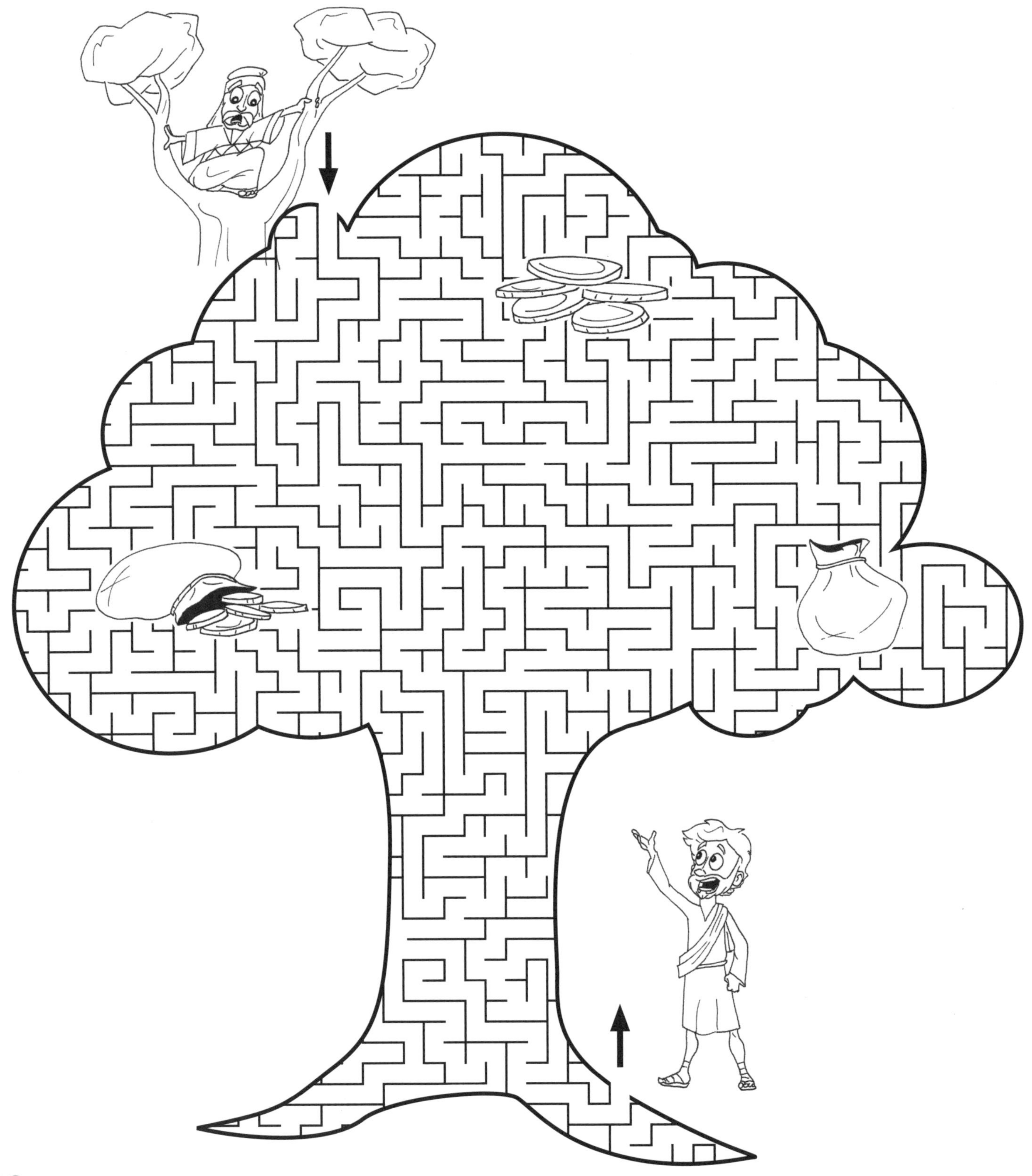

The **A-MAZE-ING** Ride

Jesus and His disciples were going to Jerusalem. Jesus sent two disciples into a village to get a donkey for Him to ride. A large crowd gathered and spread their cloaks on the road for Jesus to ride over. Some cut palm branches and waved them, shouting, "Hosanna! Blessed is he who comes in the name of the Lord!"

Help the happy crowd reach Jesus. Watch out for the palm branches!

The **A-MAZE-ING** Sacrifice of Jesus

Some religious leaders hated Jesus. They made up lies about Him and had Jesus arrested. Even though the judge knew Jesus had done nothing wrong, he sent Him away to be crucified. Jesus died on the cross to save us from our sins. A Roman centurion, who saw what happened, said, "Surely this man was the Son of God!"

Help the centurion reach Jesus. Watch out for the thorns!

The **A-MAZE-ING** Resurrection of Jesus

After Jesus died, Joseph of Arimathea asked the judge for Jesus' body. He wrapped the body in a clean linen cloth and laid it in his own new tomb. Then Joseph rolled a big stone in front of the door. After the Sabbath, some women came to the tomb and saw the stone rolled away. An angel told them, "Jesus has risen!" Jesus was alive again!

Help the women reach the angel. Be careful not to drop any spices along the way!

The **A-MAZE-ING** Return to Heaven

Jesus appeared to His disciples. He even showed them His nail scars. Jesus told them to go and preach the gospel, to baptize believers, and to teach people to obey Jesus' commands. Jesus promised to be with them always. Then He arose to heaven. The disciples returned to the city to begin their work for Jesus with joyful hearts.

Help the disciples see Jesus as He is taken up to heaven.

ANSWER KEY

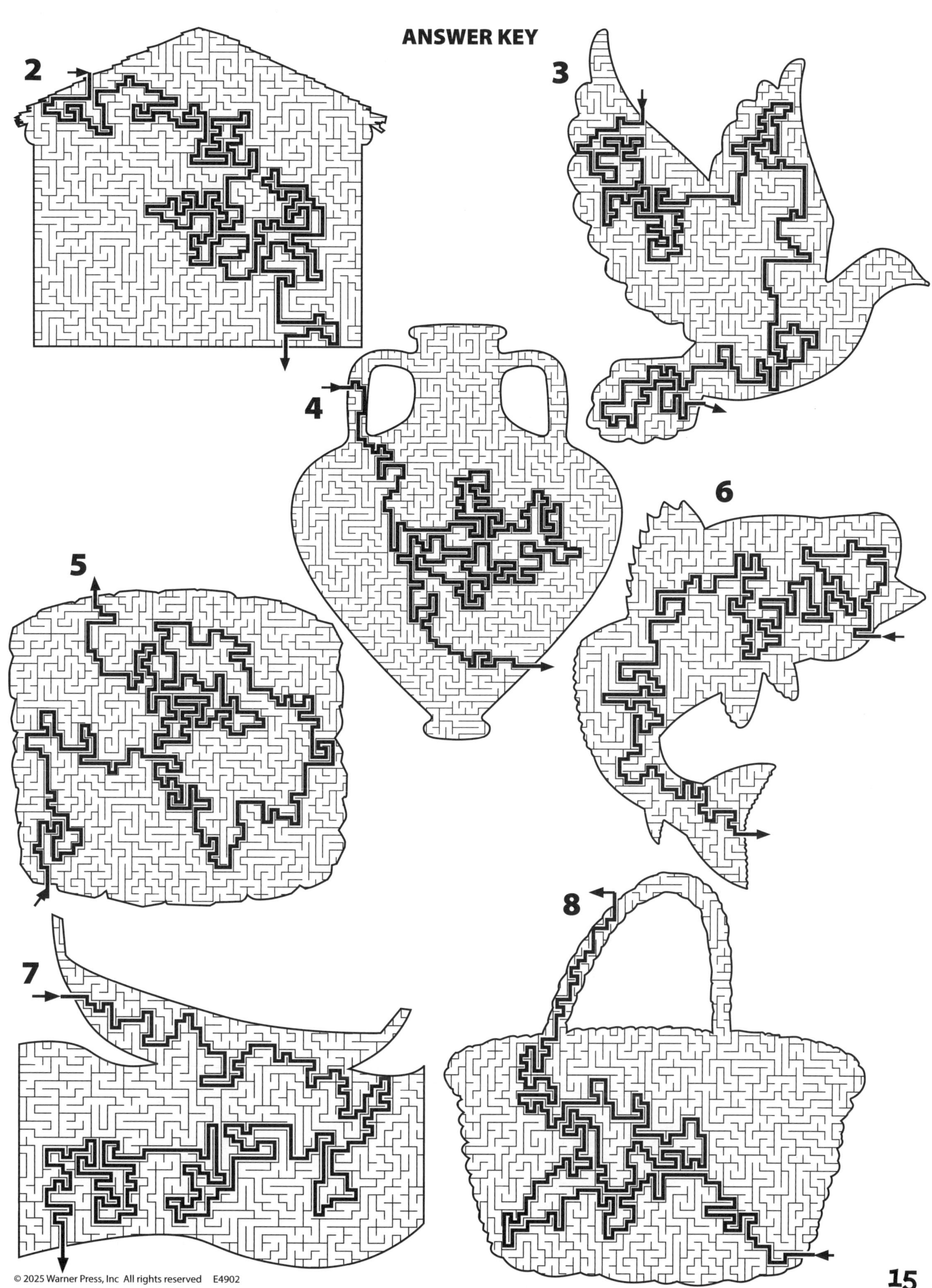

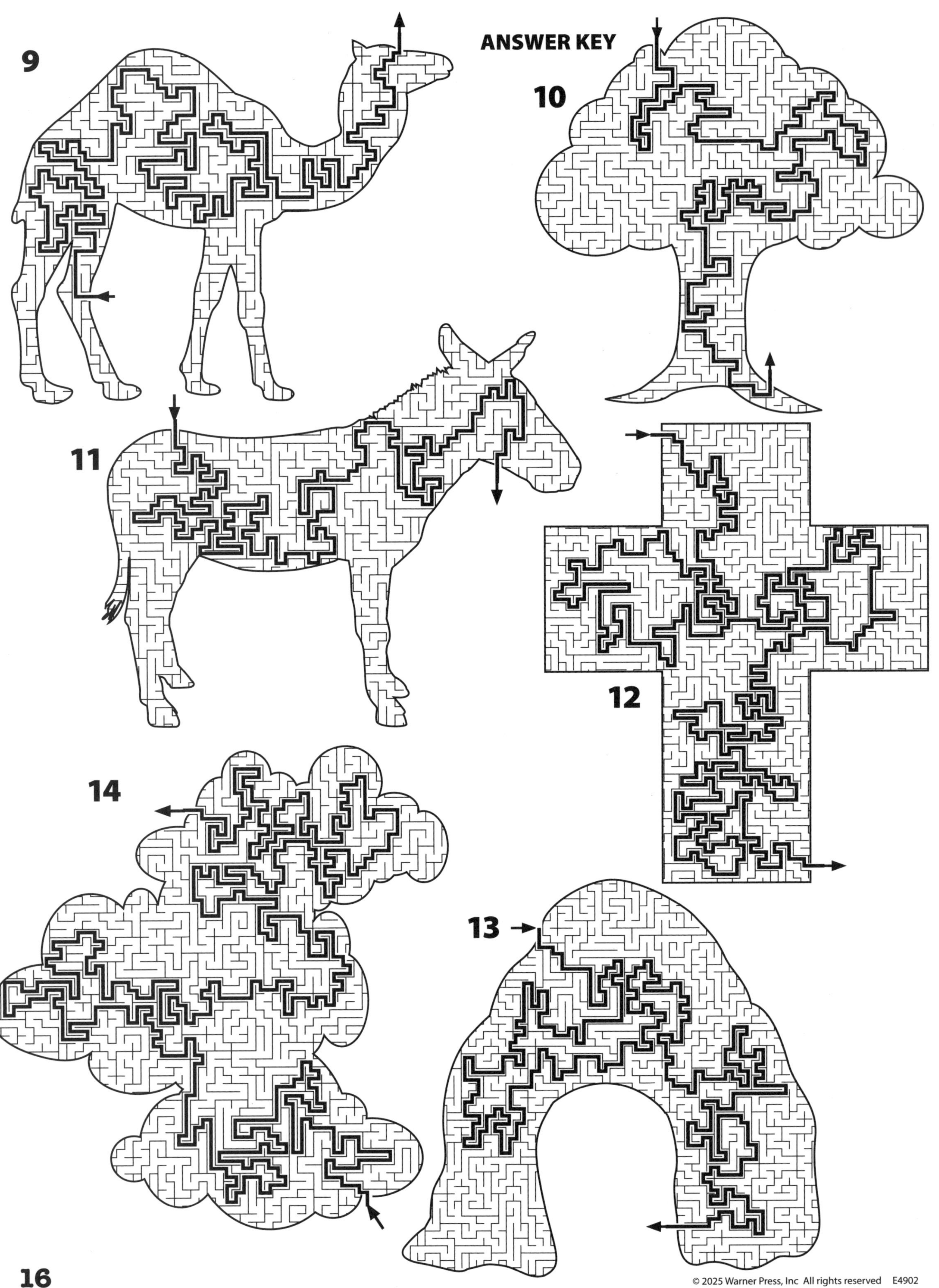
ANSWER KEY
9
10
11
12
13
14